ESS

DIALECT

A Selection of Essex
Words and Anecdotes

by
Camilla Zajac

BRADWELL
BOOKS

Published by Bradwell Books
9 Orgreave Close Sheffield S13 9NP
Email: books@bradwellbooks.co.uk

British Library Cataloguing in Publication Data:
a catalogue record for this book is available from the
British Library.

1st Edition

ISBN: 9781902674674

Print: Gomer Press, Llandysul, Ceredigion SA44 4JL

Design by: Andrew Caffrey

Image Credits: Unless otherwise stated all images
reproduced by courtesy of the Essex Record Office.

INTRODUCTION

Today when you mention Essex to a person, their first association is often with the hit TV programme, The Only Way Is Essex. Yet there is a whole lot more to Essex, as is revealed by this brief look at the county's dialect.

The journey of researching this book has been a great reminder of the delight of the words that define a place – whether it is the vibrant language of the dialect poem John Noakes & Mary Styles or the evocative names of some of the traditional dishes of the area! They are all reminders that distance creates dialect. This means both the distant history recorded word for word in the language of a place and the geographical distance that creates sharp distinctions between the everyday words of one place and another. It is this distance – and dialect – that makes the world a more interesting place, as any 'furriner' (see glossary) reading this book will hopefully discover!

It has been fascinating to learn about 'new' old words such as 'blatherskite' and 'goffle' and to find out what a 'fire-cat' was once used for! It is also intriguing to see how certain turns of phrase may have their roots in the people and places of Essex. Yet even when this is fiction rather than fact, it reveals a great deal about the past and how we see it. For example, while the link between Old King Cole and Colchester may only be an appealing myth, it still tells a fascinating story.

As you will see, there is a great deal to the language behind Essex, far more than this book could ever cover. Much as I would have liked to have explored more deeply, this book provides just a brief - but hopefully colourful - look at the words and sayings created by the history of this county. Read on to see what you can discover about the dialect and past of Essex! Thank you to Essex Record Office for their help with my research for this book.

Camilla Zajac

A

Abear - to endure

Adry - thirsty

Afeared - scared

Agin - against

A goo - ago

A-goon - a-going

Ails - ears of corn

Aint - are not

Aldoe - although

Alma chizzit - how much is it?

Amant - amount

A-mos - almost

Andraa - a clown, a mountebank

Anoather - another

Anough - enough

Argify/argufy - argue

Ark - clouds running into two points

Arly - early

Arter - after

Arterwards - afterwards

Artnoon - afternoon

Assband - housebound

Ast - asked

Attact - attack

A-tome - at home

Aukard - awkward

Awss - horse

Ax'd - asked

B

Bag - to cut plants with a hook

Bagging hook - a sickle-shaped tool with an angled blade

Ballet - ballad

Bange - light rain

Bargun - began

Barmed up - mud covered

Barn work - a threshing machine

Beat out - puzzled, put in a quandary

Beaver ploughmans - packed lunch

Behine - behind

Beilywengins - small or sour beer

Bellar - to bellow, cry out violently

Bettermust - best (only to describe clothes)

Bever - a farm labourer's lunch

Bigge - cow's teat

Bile - boil

Biling - the whole number

Bine - stem of a climbing plant,
now more often of potatoes

Bin - been

Biznus - business

Bizzy - busy

Blab - to tell secrets, talk

Blare - to cry, to weep aloud

Blatherskite - a person who is boastful

Blunt - money

Boarnt - bonnet

Bobbish - pretty well in health

Bobs - shillings

Boddle - bottle

Boine - swelling

Bonie - blow or wound

Bonkka - very large

Bonx- to beat up mix for batter puddings

Bote - bought

Bouy - boy

Brads - money

Bran-new, and **bran-span-new** - quite new

Britches - breeches

Broom - the name of a plant used to make brooms

Brote - brought

Bruck - broke

Bullimong - a combination of oats, vetch and peas

Bumby - place where household rubbish is placed

Bum-by - by and by

Bumpy hole - a cess pit
Bunting - untidy dress
Busk - to lie in sun
Buss - to kiss, to embrace
By gom! - an exclamation

Off to class we go: school children travelling by horse and cart at Ford End in Great Waltham.

C

Caint - can not
Call - occasion, need
Cammicks - left over food
Carl - curl
Cart rake - cart track

Charmber - chamber

Chap - a man, a fellow

Chap rein - leading rein for a horse

Charriter - character

Chaseway - private road leading to a farm or field

Chate - a feast, a treat

Chaw - to chew

Chevy - to chase, to run after

Chice - small portion

Chimbley - chimney

Chine - to chop ribs of beef halfway through

Chitterlings - small intestines of a pig, cooked as food

Choat - a yearling pig.

Chop - the lips

Chubby - ruddy, full-faced, healthy

Chuck full - quite full, crammed

Chutch - church

Claa - claw

Close - sultry, still weather

Clumsy–thump - a heavy blow

Clungy - description for wet heavy clay soil

Coach - to drive

Coad-chill - an ague fit

Coas - course

Coffin - a big shoe

Cos - because

Count - to think, intend

Court - pig's court or hog's court. A yard adjoining a pig sty

Cow - to cower

Crazy - over-anxious, excited

Crib - to rob

Cried-up - well spoken of, much praised

Croat - a field

Crope - to grope, to walk cautiously

Cross-grained - troublesome, cross, awry

Crotch - a fork in a tree

Crotch tail - kite

Crumbles - crumbs

Cruppy - bad tempered

Cubs - children (generally used contemptuously)

Cuddy - hedge sparrow

Cue - humour, temper

Cuff - to try to make believe, to insinuate

Culch - rubbish of any description

Cunning - knowing or clever

Curosity - curiosity

Curous - curious

Cuss - curse

Cut away - to move away or get in with things quickly

Cute - sharp, clever

D

Dabster - a very capable person

Dag - dew

Dang it - an exclamation, not used angrily

Dan in the maff - down in the mouth

Dapster - an adept or proficient person

Dart - dirt

Darter - daughter

Dare - to grieve

Dash my buttons! - an exclamation

Dawdling - trifling, idling

Dean - din or noise

Deadly - superlative of anything, as deadly good

Ded - did

Dent - did not

Desarves - deserves

Deviltry - devilry

Dicky - donkey, ass

Dibbler - pointed stick for making holes for seed planting

Dif - deaf

Dilvered - exhausted, worn out with fatigue

Directly - now, immediately

Disannul - to do away with, to disturb

Do - to work for as a charwoman

Doe - do

Dogged way - a great way, excessive

Dogs - dew

Doke - a small brook or a bruise

Donkey's years - long ago

Dollop - large spoonful

Dool - unploughed boundary strip across a field

Draa - draw

Draffs - drawings, pictures

Drean - to drain

Dreening wet - soaked by rain

Dreft - drove

Drink by word of mouth - to drink straight from the bottle

Dubs - money

Dullar - an uninterrupted noise, confusion

Dullerin - to cry

Dumps - low spirits

Dunt - to confuse by noise

Dutch barn - a barn with open sides

E

Eand - the end

East - yeast

Eel thing - St Elmo's Fire

Ees - yes

Eke out - to use sparingly

Elbow-grease - hard work done with hands

Elevens(es) - a meal between meals enjoyed by labourers at haytime or harvest

Enow - enough

Essex stile - ditch

Etch - each, every one

Every etch - every other

Expect - to suppose

Eye - to observe closely

Eye-eels - high heels

Workers at Bulford Mill in Cressing

F

Fairing - a present bought at a fair

Fared - felt, seemed

Favour - to resemble personally

Feff - to buy or sell too much

Fell - to come round periodically

Fellar - fellow

Fidgit - restless, uneasy

Fills - fields

Fimble - to touch lightly

Fine - find

Fire-cat - a wooden tool used for keeping plates warm in front of a fire

Fit - sufficient, enough

Flacked - hung loose, agitated by the wind

Flaring - very bright, gaudy

Flavour - to taste

Flee - to skin

Fleck - the fur of a rabbit or other furry animal

Flummergasted - astonished

Foce - force

Following time - a season in which fine weather and showers follow each other in quick succession

Foreigner - individual from another county or district

Fours(es) - a meal between meals enjoyed by labourers at harvest (see Elevenses)

Four way want - crossroads

Frail basket - a shapeless flexible mat basket without bottom or handle

Fresh - almost drunk

Frickle - to fidget

Frins - friends

Frize - freeze

Frum - from

Fudder - further

Furnitade - furniture

Furriner - person from outside Essex

Fust - first

G

Gab - idle talk, nonsense

Gal - girl

Gallows - T shaped iron on front of a horse drawn plough

Games - tricks, jokes

Gammy - diseased

Gammicking - gossiping, idling

Gammock - clever

Garyboy - a man who drives a sporty, done up car

Gawm - to look idly about, awkward

Gentily - gently

Ginnick - perfect

Git - get

Glare - a fixed or wild look

Glarmed up - covered in dirt

Glum - gloomy, sour, grave

Go after - to court

Goff - a mow of hay

Goffer - to eat your food very fast

Goffle - to eat fast and greedily

Goings-on - proceedings

Gole - prominent

Gomes - gums

Goo - go

Goodish way - a great way

Goosegog - gooseberry

Gownd - gown

Grab - to lay hands on

Grizzle - to complain or whimper

Growl - grumble, murmur

Grubs - toils continually

Grumble - to murmur, to be discontented

Grunsops - tea grounds

Grutch - to grumble

Gud - good

Gulch - to fall heavily

Gulching - a big rain downpour

Gullion - a stomach-ache
Gumption - nonsense, foolish talk
Gut - got
Guzzle - drink

Dagenham in the old days: a watercolour showing
Dagenham in around 1900

H

Ha - have
Haa't - have it
Hafe - half
Hainish - unpleasant
Half tidy - good
Hallarbaloo - a great noise, a tumult

Hames - the iron fittings on a horses collar for attaching the traces

Hampered - perplexed, annoyed

Hand - a signature

Hanger - to desire, to long for

Hankerchar - handkerchief

Har - her

Hard - heard

Hare-brained - giddy, thoughtless

Harum-scarum - thoughtless, giddy

Harve - a haw

Haysel - the hay season

Hazel - to dry

Hazle - stiff as clay

Hedge-Betty - hedge sparrow

Heft - weight

Higgle - to haggle

Hinder - yonder

Hips - the corners of a haystack

Hoap - helped

Hoddemedod - snail

Hockey - the harvest-home supper

Hobble - a scrape, a difficulty

Hobbly - uneven, rough

Hope - an enclosed piece of land

Hoppet - a small meadow close to habitation for resting sick animals

Hoss - horse
Housen - houses
Howsomever - however
Hued - held
Huffers - bread rolls
Huiliday - holiday
Hulk - a heavy fall
Hull - to throw
Hum - stink
Humoursome - courteous
Hump - a great amount
Hunks - a miser
Hunt - had not
Hutch - a chest, a large box

I

Independent - of no occupation, retired
Inquiration - an inquiry
Intossicated - intoxicated
Itched - felt anxious

J

Jacob - a frog
Jack in - to give up
Jackanips - an affected puppyish young man

Jagger - to talk noisily
Jar - to scold
Jarney - journey
Jice - a small amount
Jigger - an axe
Jocoshus - jocose, merry
Joggle - a shaking
Jolly - footpath or track often between hedges
Joulterhead - a blockhead, a clown
Jounce - a jolt
Jub - a very slow trot
Julk - a hard blow, a jolt

K

Keeping Room - living room
Kept company - courted
Kicksey - a large hollow stemmed plant
Kick-the-buckit - to die
Kickshaws - trifles, fancy cakes
Kilters - tools, instruments
Kissing gate - small gate in an angular enclosure
Kit - a great number
Kitch - catch
Kittle - kettle
Kivered - covered

Knaa - know
Knocked up - worn out with fatigue
Knowed - knew

L

Lamed - learned
Las - last
Leaf - leave
Leap - movable barrier below barn doors
Lear - to scowl, to frown
Learn - to teach
Leas –ways - at least
Leetle - little
Lickerty-split - at full speed
Liddle - little
Liggle - to struggle while carrying something too heavy
Little scrailes - naughty little children
List of hearing - ready, quick
Looker - a bailiff
Loave - love
Lollipops - a sweet lozenge made of treacle, butter and flour
Look at the nose - to seem out of temper, to frown
Lord - lord of the harvest, leader of a reaping gang at harvest time.

Lozenger - a lozenge
Lugsome - heavy
Lunnon - London
Lush - loosely rooted

M

Maggots - whims, strange fancies
Make a noise - to scold, to be angry with
Make count - to intend
Mayhap - perhaps, it may happen
Martlemas beef - beef dried in the chimney
Marm - a stuck up individual
Mauther - awkward girl
Meller - miller
Mess of - serving of
Mew - mowed, cut with a scythe
Mind - to remember
Mizzle - to give up
Molloncholy - melancholy
Mooch - to lurk about
Morrar - morrow
Mort - a great number, many
Moorish - tasty
Mosly - mostly
Muckinger - handkerchief

Muggy - half drunk
Muller - butterfly
Mulligrubs - imagined illnesses, ill humours
Mum - silent, secret anger

N

Naa - no
Naarbour - neighbour
Narrow-wriggle - an earwig
Nation - many, much
Nettled - provoked, disturbed
Newing - yeast
Nipped up - hard up
Nippet - small quantity
Noggin - small quantity of drink
None-or-both - neither
Not - well tiled
Noteless - stupefied
Nut - not
Nuver - never
Nuzzle - sound of bellows

O

Oad - old

Oaf - off

Oather - other

Obstropolus - obstreperous

Od rabbet! - an exclamation not used angrily

Of afire - on fire

Ollis - always

Old fashioned - cunning

Ollust - always

Onsensed - shocked

Ood - would

Orfan - often

Osier - willow for basket making

Out of heart - low spirited

Out of the way - extravagant

Oven Builder - a long tailed tit

Over-night - the night previous

Owd - old

Own - to acknowledge

The Essex pig or Sus bucculentus which is thought to originate from Essex. While up until quite recently this type of pig was officially extinct, breeders are now trying to bring it back into popularity.
Morphart Creation/ShutterStock

P

Parkey - feeling cold
Parish lantern - the moon
Peg - legs or feet
Peggles - Cowslips
Pennorth - a pennyworth
Perished - very cold
Phthisickin - a tickly cough
Piggatory - great trouble
Pightle - a small grass field near a house
Pike - a pitchfork
Pitch - to load up straw on a waggon
Pitch a pennie pie - somersault
Plum pudding - the Red Campion flower
Poke up with - to have to put up with
Pollywagtail - tadpoles
Prong - a fork
Puggle - to poke about
Puss - purse

Q

Quackled - choked
Quarters - the spaces between the horse track and the wheel ruts
Queer - feeling ill
Quinny - not quite, not just yet

Quire - inquire

Quoite - quite

R

Racks - range, kitchen fire-place

Raddle - to place sticks into a hedge to strengthen it

Rainbow - a field ploughed in curves

Rapscallion - a rascal

Rassle - to stir the embers in an oven with a pole

Ratty - angry

Rays and jags - tatters, worn-out dress

Rayther - rather

Releet - a crossing of roads

Rench - to rinse out a cloth

Render - to melt down fat

Rep - reaped

Retch - reach

Ridding - an area cleared of trees to create a new field or meadow

Right matty - looking untidy

Right on - violently

Riled - made angry, disturbed

Rip - tool used for hedging

Roll - to wheel along

Rub - a stone for sharpening tools

Ruff - roof
Ruinated - decayed, gone to ruin
Rum - odd, uncommon
Rumpus - a great noise, a row
Runty - surly

S

Saa - saw
Sarce - vegetables
Sarteny - certainly
Scallion - an onion planted out after winter storing and eaten raw
Scaly - shabby, mean
Scamp - a rascal
Scat - scared
Scatch pawed - left handed
Scringing - cringing
Scroivdge - a crowd, a squeeze
Sen - since
Shaint - shall not
Shaw - a small wood
Sheu - showed
Shood or Shewed - showed or show
Shot - a piece of land
Shoont - should not

Short-coated - short tempered

Shot - money

Shud - should

Shut knife - a pocket knife

Sich - such

Sight - a great number

Sing-small - having to put up with less than was expected

Sin - seen

Skep - a straw beehive

Slipe - a strip of land

Slummuck - to laze about

Smart as a carrot - very smart indeed

Smuck - smoke

Snacks - to share out equally

Snarl - tangle

Snaith - the handle of a scythe

Sneer - to twitch

Snew - snowed

Snib - to rub the shoots off potatoes

Snitch - the nose

Soadgers - soldiers

Sot - set or sat

Spake - spoke

Spike - the parish workhouse

Spote - sport

Spring - a small wood

Squench - quench

Squiggle - to shake about

Stale - the long handle of a pitchfork

Stetch - a ridge between furrows

Stick - an eccentric person

Stint or stent - period of work

Stone-horse - a stone-ware bottle for carrying beer.

Stooke - piled sheaves of corn

Stroke - a game

Stub - to dig up a tree stump

Stull - a big piece of bread

Stummick - stomach

Stumped - to be without money

Stumps - feet

Sub - an advance on payment for a job

Suffin - something

Suky - a kettle

Sum'dy - somebody

Summoned - given notice to appear in court

Suvrins - sovereigns

Swabble - a quarrel, loud talking

Swack - to go or hit against violently

Swiggle - to shake up liquid in a bottle or other container

T

Tag-rag and bob-tail - the rabble

Taint - isn't

Tantarums - noisy, hurly-burly

Tares - rough grass

Tedder - to turn newly mown grass

Tetchy - cross

Teuk - redshank

Tewly - poorly, not in good health

Thole-pin - pin removed to allow the cart body to tip back

Thote - thought

Thrap - to crowd

Threadle - to thread a needle

Three-square - triangular

Throat-latch - the strap under a horse's throat which holds the bridle

Thurrar - furrow

Thussins - in this way

Thusty - thirsty

Tiddy Widdy - small

Tied-up - married, united

Tifflin - small or light

Tiff - a fit of bad-temper

Tighted-up - dressed neatly, put in order

Tilt - covering for a load

Time (a time or two) - once or twice

Timmersome - timid, fearful

Tip me torter - see-saw

Tip the cash - to hand it over, pay immediately

Tiptop - at the most

Tivig - to observe slyly

Toad - told

Tommy - food carried to work (soldier's expression for ration bread)

Top latch - strap at the top of a horses collar for fastening the hames

Tore out - worn out

Toward - the near side of a wagon or horse, to the left

To-year - the current year, the present season

Tramp - to walk, to journey on foot

Trapes - to trudge

Troy - try

Truck - rubbish

Tuck - took

Twitch - couch grass

U

Uffler - a type of bargeman

Umberrelld - umbrella

Underwood - undergrowth

Upright - independent

Urn - them

Ust - used

Uster could - I could before

V

Vail - a tip

W

Wamble - to totter from one side to another

Wanckle - weak

Wants - a site where three or four roads meet

Wark - work

Warld - world

Warnxin - vermin

Warsley - not much

Well-to-do - thrifty, prosperous

Wellum - a small footbridge over a ditch

Wentersome - venturous, bold, daring

Werry - very

Weskit - waistcoat

Wet week - to feel melancholy

What - that

Whippletree - bar on a plough where the traces are placed

Whistle - the throat

Whoile - while

Wholly - altogether

Whop - a heavy severe blow

Wile heas - wild beasts

Wind - wine
Winnick - a suppressed cry, to fret
Wonderment - to hear with astonishment
Woolve - a water conduit under a road
Woor-ree - what a ploughman call to his horse for it to move to the right
Wor - were
Worses - verses
Wos-a-matter - what is the matter?
Woundly - very great
Wrap up - to place in the coffin, finished
Wringe - line of seedlings
Wusser - worse
Wust - worst

Y

Yallar - yellow
Yard - garden
Yarn - earn
Yit - yet
Yow - you

Z

Zact - exact

Essex in times gone by: Village Street, looking towards Dunmow
in Ford End, Great Waltham

A little word about The Only Way Is Essex

There's no denying that many people closely associate
Essex with the TV show The Only Way Is Essex, or it's also
affectionately known, TOWIE. TOWIE has been credited
with bringing words and phrases like "reem", "well jel" and
"shuut up" into general use. Though these might seem a
million miles away from the Essex language of the past,
some experts believe that they continue an old tradition.
Like it or not, TOWIE is part of the Essex dialect and is
fast becoming part of everyday speech even further afield!

Arrrra - hello | **Awight babe?** - hello
Reem - cool | **Shaaaaap** - please be quiet
Well jell/jel - envious |

Essex: what's in a name?

The place name Essex is believed to have come from the 'Kingdom of the East Seaxe' which means 'Kingdom of the East Saxons', created by Aescwine in 527 AD. Essex's county emblem depicts three seax. A seax was an old single-edged knife or sword.

Say what? Sayings about or from Essex

Essex has featured in a number of proverbs and sayings over the years, some familiar and others long forgotten.

Essex miles, Suffolk stiles, Norfolk wiles,
many men beguiles

This interesting old proverb aims to communicate the quirks of three different counties. The 'Essex miles' don't actually refer to a measurement of distance, but to the enclosures or fields in the county, with the message being that they were very small. The features of other counties include the small and difficult to use stiles of Suffolk and the 'wiles' of the many lawyers that were based in Norfolk in the past! It's a neat little proverb that reveals a little history about Essex and its neighbouring counties.

As wise as Walthams calf

As wise as Walthams calf, that ran nine miles to suck a bull

As wise as Walthams calf (who went nine miles to suck
a bull and came home as dry as he went)

There are several versions of this strange and now nearly forgotten saying. One interpretation of it is that it is a joke about the poor quality of the preaching done by the monks of Abbey Church of Walton Holy Cross in Waltham Abbey. We'll never know the truth for sure, but it's an interesting saying.

Braintree for the pure, and Bocking for the poor;
Cogshall for the jeering town, And Kelvedon for the whore.

This strange saying certainly sounds insulting from the outset and proves to be on closer view. The wording conveys a very negative view of each of these areas of Essex!

As valiant as an Essex lion

This analogy isn't stating that big cats once roamed the streets of Romford and other parts of Essex! The 'Essex lion' actually refers to a calf. The calves produced in the county were famed for being the finest and largest in the country.

Keeping Dovercourt: all talkers and no hearers

Keeping Dovercourt is an intriguing saying, long out of

everyday use, but with its roots in Essex. A court was held every year at Dovercourt, a small seaside town near Harwich. It was supposed to be quite a rowdy affair which is why keeping Dovercourt is said to mean making a lot of noise!

In a fox's sleep (to be in a)

Here's another saying believed to have its origins in Essex. It is meant to describe someone faking a state of sleep - that is, a person who pretends to be asleep while actually listening to the words of the people around them!

Forwhy

In use (at least in books) until the end of the 17th century, this Essex saying could be seen as a precursor of the saying "And I'll tell you for why" which is still used today!

Giving the straight tip

Thought to hail from rural parts of Essex, this saying means to give a person a clear message about something and not to let them get away with anything in the process!

Go to Romford to have your backsides new bottomed

This rather strange saying makes perfect sense when you know about Romford's history as a centre for breeches-making. Breeches were a type of trouser and Romford was the place to get them many years ago!

Hard at work: Farm workers harvesting corn at Hill Farm,
Ford End in Great Waltham

Good elm, good barley; good oak, good wheat

Here's another Essex saying which holds a little of the
region's history in a few words - this time, of farming.

Lying by the wall

This euphemistic saying refers to someone who is dead, but
not yet buried!

**When the moon is at the full, mushrooms you may
freely pull; but when the moon is on the wane, wait ere
you think to pluck again**

This old piece of folklore is said to originate from Essex. It gives
clear instructions about the best time to pick mushrooms,
something that the people of Essex and elsewhere would once
have followed, due to their belief in the power of the moon!

Put the millers eye out

When you put the miller's eye out, you water down a food or pudding with too much water or milk! This strange Essex saying is also believed to refer to mixing mortar.

Ugly church, ugly steeple; ugly parson, ugly people.

This harsh saying is said to refer to the village of Ugley in Essex!

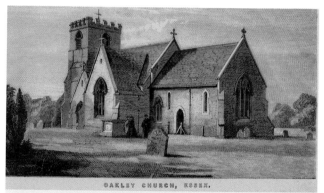

OAKLEY CHURCH, ESSEX.

Not so **'Ugley'** after all: Ugley Church
The caption on the print says 'Oakley Church'.
This isn't a mistake. It's because the place name gradually became
corrupted from **Oakley** to **Ugley!**

Like billy-o

Most of us have heard or used this saying at some point. It comes with a few possible interpretations. One is said to be about Joseph Billio, an 18th century Puritan preacher who was based at the United Reformed Church in Market Hill in Maldon, in the late 1600s. Because of his extreme style of preaching, Billio was considered to be the inspiration behind this saying. However, there are other interpretations, for example, that the saying was actually a more polite way of referring to the devil. But in Maldon, Joseph Billio is still thought to be the person behind the saying and there is a plaque in the town to say so!

Bring home the bacon

This saying is still in use today and means to earn money or to be financially successful. It has been closely linked to the Dunmow Flitch trials.

A little history about the Dunmow Flitch

The Dunmow Flitch is an Essex tradition which continues right up to the present day. It started in 1104AD 1104 at the Augustinian Priory of Little Dunmow when the Lord and Lady of the Manor (Reginald Fitzwalter and his wife) dressed up plainly to disguise themselves as poor folk and asked for the blessing of the Prior a year and a day after their marriage. This impressed the Prior so much that he gave them a flitch of bacon ('flitch' is the local word for a side of bacon - actually half a pig cut sideways).

Celebrating marital harmony: Thomas and Ann Shakeshaft claim
the Flitch of Bacon at Little Dunmow

Once he had revealed his identity, Fitzwalter bestowed his land to the priory on the condition that a flitch was awarded to any other couple in England who could say truthfully that they had enjoyed complete marital harmony for the preceding year and a day! Over the years, the tradition grew, was forgotten, then was restarted again. It is even referred to in Geoffrey Chaucer's The Wife of Bath's Tale and Prologue! Entrants must satisfy the judge and jury of "six maidens and six bachelors that in 'twelvemonth and a day', they have 'not wisht themselves unmarried again'. The winners will then 'bring home the bacon'!

The tradition of the Dunmow Flitch has survived so well into the modern age that it even has its own website. You can read more about its history at **www.dunmowflitchtrials.co.uk!**

Geoffrey Chaucer (1343-1400) who mentioned the tradition of the Dunmow Flitch in The Wife of Bath's Tale and Prologue.

Georgios Kollidas/Shutterstock

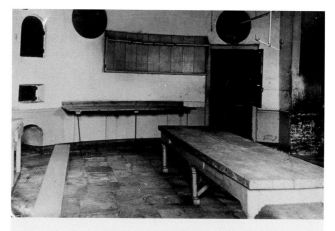

Another world: the kitchen at Gidea Hall in Romford

Fob off

This everyday phrase means to be put off with something inferior. It may have its roots in a political rebellion in a small village in Essex. The story which links the saying with the village goes like this:

In 1381, John Brampton, the king's tax collector, went into the Essex village of Fobbing. His mission? To collect the poll tax of three groats from every one of the local villagers. However, the villagers worked as a group to resist this and succeeded in sending Brampton away, or fobbing him off! This was the start of the Peasant's Revolt in England!

A view of the village of Fobbing from the creek

There are arguments that the verb 'fob' was only in use in its current meaning a couple of centuries after Brampton was sent away from Fobbing. So this may well be a great story rather than a saying which really originated in Essex.

Epitaph for an Essex miller

Here lies an honest miller, and that is Strange
Epitaph on Essex churchyard of a miller named Strange

This famous epitaph is a real one from the gravestone of an Essex miller. It speaks for the fact that many years ago, millers were popularly considered dishonest due to disputes about measurements!

Unusual Essex place names

Naughty, odd or downright peculiar, these are all real place names in Essex!

- Bachelors Bump
- Pork Lane
- Turkey Cock Lane
- Ugley
- Chignall Smealy
- Fingringhoe
- Good Easter
- Layer-de-la-Haye
- Messing

A taste of Essex

Essex dishes were often as distinctive as the local dialect. These were the food names - and dishes - on people's lips!

Oysters

For many centuries, Essex was famed for its oysters which provided an affordable and delicious source of food in dishes such as smoked oyster parcels. Oysters were also an important source of employment. They were in abundant supply right up until the late 1800s when disease and price competition affected stocks.

The oyster:
an important part of
Essex's past and present
Morphart Creation/Shutterstock

Colchester Natives and the Oyster Feast

While in many parts of Essex, the availability - and consumption - of oysters has sadly decreased over the years, it continues in other areas.

Essex oysters come from some of the finest oyster waters in the world. Some waters cannot be accessed by people or industry, making them pollution-free.

Colchester is the heart of Essex oyster growing. In fact, the Colchester Oyster Fishery supplies some of most prestigious restaurants in Britain, including Le Gavroche, The Ritz in London and Gordon Ramsey's restaurants! The oyster fishery in Colne dates right back to the Roman age. Its oysters are famously known as 'Colchester Natives'. They are harvested from September to May in the area off Mersea Island.

In 1189, Richard I granted the Borough a charter giving it control of the fishery with the aim of raising revenue and to control the harvesting of oysters off Mersea Island. This control has continued to varying degrees over the following 800 years. While the dredgers took all the revenue, the authorities appealed to the law to regain some of the profits at the end of the 19th century. Nowadays, the Colne fishery is officially opened every year with a special ritual on the water featuring the Mayor of Colchester!

As part of the event, a proclamation dating back to 1256 is read by the Chief Executive, restating the claim to the fishery rights.

The Mayor then dredges the first oyster, which he or she then consumes. Intriguingly, a toast is then drunk in gin, accompanied by a piece of gingerbread. No-one knows exactly why this is done, but it's part of a very old tradition!

Another important date in the local diary is the Oyster Feast on the last Friday of October.

Boiled Eels

These fishy delicacies were in abundant supply in Essex. So it's no surprise that dishes such as boiled eels were on the menu for many locals!

Ginger Pudding

Essex locals enjoyed ginger pudding because not only was it delicious and filling, it was also cheap to make!

Swish-Swash

This was the unusual name of an alcohol drink or mead made in Essex (and some other areas) which combined honeycomb, water, pepper and other spices.

Essex Epping Sausages

Ask for a plate of Essex Epping Sausages and you would get a delicious dish of skinless pork sausages seasoned with a good mix of herbs and spices, including nutmeg, marjoram, sage and thyme as well as lemon zest.

Farm worker **Charles Sweeting** enjoying a break in around 1890.

These sausages were said to taste of venison and it was suggested that venison was secretly added into the sausage mix to give it its unique taste!

Essex Pea Soup

If you really wanted to experience a traditional pea soup from Essex, you would need to sieve your peas through a hair sieve, known as a 'Tammy' cloth.

Essex Spice Cakes

It is believed that these cakes, which were packed with fruit and spices, were created to mark a local religious feast day. They were usually made with rosewater, a common ingredient right up to the 20th century.

Ongar Ham Cake

A cake made from ham? This delicacy is thought to be traditional to Ongar. It was made of cooked minced ham and bread soaked in ale and seasonings, all held together with egg. It was also thought to have been baked in a water bath.

Harwich Kitchels

These delicacies are connected with an ancient tradition in which each new Mayor of Harwich throws kitchels from the window of the Guildhall to waiting children in the street below. Kitchels were in fact a type of small spiced bun. The 400 year old ceremony was started as a way of spreading good will by helping the poor of the town and continues to this day!

Saffron Cake

What could be more traditional to Essex than a cake made using probably its most well known herb? Saffron actually gave the town of Saffron Walden the first part of its name (before that, it was known as Chipping Walden). Saffron was traditionally used to flavour buns and cakes like the traditional Essex Saffron Cake.

Essex Cockle Soup

Cockles have long been associated with Essex. Today, it is thought that the UK's best cockles are to be found in Leigh-on-Sea, Essex! Traditional Essex Cockle Soup celebrates this very local seafood with a mix of cockles, bacon, white wine and parsley.

Asparagus Pudding

A pudding is not something we would normally associate with asparagus. But in the 19th century, it was enjoyed by people in Essex. Think of a subtly flavoured kind of bread pudding. Sounds delicious!

Colchester Pudding

Unlike Asparagus Pudding, this native Colchester pudding is a sweet treat, containing tapioca, cream, stewed fruit and topped off with meringue. But this was a pudding with a purpose. Apparently created around 1850, it was served up at formal civic events.

Cranham Honey Cake

This sweet delicacy originated, as the name reveals, in Cranham (which was first known as Bishops Ockendon) and includes lemon peel and glacé cherries.

Barley Cream Soup

Essex was an important barley growing area in the 18th century. Barley Cream Soup celebrated this fact and provided people with a delicious dish based around their local crop.

Essex lions

Essex was so famed for its beef during the 18th and 19th centuries that cattle were referred to as 'Essex lions' while people from the county were known as 'Essex calves'!

Other Essex dishes from the past include:

Milk soup · **Oyster soup** · **Southend whitebait**
Dunmow chitterling turnovers · **Rook pie**
Oxbird pudden · **Turnip bread** · **Scrap buns**
Cockle cakes · **Saffron wigs** · **Candied eryngo**

An essential ingredient

The East coast of Essex has been the source of one of our most vital ingredients for more than 2000 years. This part of the county was once a key site for harvesting salt from the sea and was right at the core of the salt making industry. The long standing salt industry has shaped the identity of the area with place names such as Salcotte, Gore Saltings and Saltcote Hall. While most of the salt making industry has now ceased in Essex, it continues to this day in Maldon.

Ford and Dagenham: a long history

How did Essex become so closely associated with one of the biggest car brands in the world? It all began in Dagenham in 1931 when car company Ford opened what was Britain and Europe's largest car plant at the time. Built on old marshlands, the first Ford built on the site was the Model AA truck. In 1939, the plant focused on producing resources for the war effort, producing no less than 360,000 light vans, army trucks, Ford V8-powered Bren Gun carriers and other vehicles and equipment! In fact, the Dagenham site was responsible for 95% of Britain's tractor production for the extra agricultural work required to support the war effort! The site grew even bigger in the fifties with floor space increasing by 50% and a doubling in production rates. By 1953 the site occupied four million square feet and employed 40,000 local people! It was in the 60s that the Dagenham site started producing what was affectionately known as the 'Dagenham Dustbin' – the Ford Cortina! The plant ended up making three million altogether.

It was also in the 1960s that the Dagenham plant became the centre of a famous strike by local women working as sewing machinists. Their protest about unequal pay led to a three-week strike and the creation of the 1970 Equal Pay Act which has improved life for countless female workers ever since.

A 1950's Ford Prefect at the Classic Car & Motorcycle Show at Cressing Temple on July 19th 2009. The Ford Prefect was the first Ford vehicle designed in the UK. Helen Shorey/ShutterStock

In 2000, it looked as though the long history shared by Ford and Essex was due to cease when it was revealed that vehicle assembly was to end at the site. In 2002, the assembly lines stopped running. In its long track record of 71 years, the Dagenham plant had built 10,980,368 cars, trucks and tractors!

However, the story of Dagenham and Ford doesn't quite end

there. The site's press shop and transport works were then added to with more engine facilities. The Dagenham Diesel Centre, Ford's centre of excellence for diesel engineering, opened in 2003. Sadly, the latest chapter in the story is that Ford is to close its stamping operation at the site. But the company has said that it will invest in a new diesel engine range at Dagenham. Whatever the future holds, it is clear that Dagenham will always play a big part in the history of one of the world's best known car brands.

Chelmsford: A first in British broadcasting history

Essex became forever associated with broadcasting history in June 15 1920. This was the date on which Marconi, the innovative 'wireless' manufacturer, made Britain's first live public entertainment broadcast from Chelmsford. The historic broadcast was made from the company's New Street plant and featured Australian soprano, Dame Nellie Melba. It involved the use of two 450 feet (140 m) radio broadcasting masts and is thought to have been received as far away as Newfoundland! The company first began its association with Essex in 1899, when Guglielmo Marconi opened the world's first 'wireless' factory under the name The Marconi Wireless Telegraph & Signal Company in Hall Street, Chelmsford. The company went on to be renamed the Marconi Wireless Telegraph Company Ltd.

In 1912, the company moved to its New Street Works. This was the site from which the first official publicised sound broadcast in the United Kingdom was made. Then in 1922, the world's first regular entertainment broadcasts began from the Marconi laboratories at Writtle, near Chelmsford. Sadly, the New Street site fell into disrepair and was finally demolished and sold to a developer in 2013. Despite this, it is clear that Essex will always hold an important place in the history of broadcasting.

Looking for bargains: a hand-coloured postcard photograph of Chelmsford Market, looking along Market Road in around 1895

Colchester: nursery rhyme city?

Faces from the past: school children from the village
of Takeley in around 1900

Colchester is said to be the oldest recorded town in Britain.
It is also believed to be the inspiration behind two of the
world's best known nursery rhymes!

Old King Cole

Old King Cole was a merry old soul,
And a merry old soul was he;
He called for his pipe,
And he called for his bowl,
And he called for his fiddlers three.
Every fiddler, he had a fiddle,
And a very fine fiddle had he;

Twee tweedle dee, tweedle dee, went the fiddlers.
Oh, there's none so rare,
As can compare
With King Cole and his fiddlers three!

Famous for being a 'merry old soul', Old King Cole has been a familiar nursery rhyme figure for many years. The roots of this popular rhyme may go all the way back to Colchester in the third century. There are actually three contenders for the honour of being the inspiration for this jolly character - all Celtic kings who went by the name of Coel. The strongest contender is thought to be the King of Colchester who was believed to living in Colchester (once the capital city of England and formerly known as Camulodunum) in the third century. It seems that the story is based on a tale from the Medieval age which aimed to bring to life the name of the city and its Roman ruins.

The legend is that the King had a daughter called Helena, who became the mother of the first Christian Roman Emperor, Constantine the Great. This also explains why St. Helena is the Patron Saint of Colchester. While the name Colchester can be read to mean 'Cole's castle', it is generally believed to come from the River Coln, named after the Roman colony. King Coel's palace is thought to have been located at the site of the Temple of Claudius which is where Colchester Castle is built. There is also an old Roman quarry in Colchester called 'King Cole's Kitchen'.

Despite the story of this 'King Cole', there is still a lot of doubt about whether Old King Cole really did originate in third century Colchester. But the legend certainly makes for interesting reading and reveals some fascinating things about Colchester's past!

Humpty Dumpty

Humpty Dumpty sat on a wall,
Humpty Dumpty had a great fall.
All the king's horses and all the king's men
Couldn't put Humpty together again.

Colchester is also believed to be the source of the story behind Humpty Dumpty, the popular egg-shaped nursery rhyme character. One theory behind the nursery rhyme is that is about a real-life cannon named Humpty Dumpty which was kept on Colchester's fortified walls!

During the English Civil war, Oliver Cromwell was attempting to take over Colchester, one of the final Royalist strongholds. He put the city under siege for no less than eleven months. The city's strong stone Roman walls helped to protect it from the Parliamentarian advance. Humpty Dumpty was brought up and placed on the wall, which was part of the church roof of the Church of St Mary's. Months and months of attempts to break down the wall followed. Finally, a hole was made in the wall below the cannon and Humpty Dumpty did indeed come falling down. The Royalists ('all the king's men') did try to put Humpty Dumpty together again by moving it to another part of the wall. But this proved impossible due to its weight! The Parliamentarians went on to take over Colchester in 1648.

Of course, this isn't the only theory behind the story of Humpty Dumpty, but it's certainly a very convincing one. It also brings to life an important part of Essex history.

Humpty Dumpty: a historical timeline

June 15 1648 - St Mary's Church in Colchester is fortified and a large cannon, Humpty Dumpty, is placed on the roof.

July 14/July 15th 1648 - The Royalist fort in the walls at St Mary's church is destroyed, along with their main cannon.

August 28th 1648 - The Royalists open the gates of Colchester and surrender to the Parliamentarians.

The star from Chipping Ongar

It's a well known and well loved English lullaby and nursery rhyme which has been sung by countless children. Yet not many people know that Twinkle Twinkle Little Star has a strong link with the Essex town of Chipping Ongar.

The song is based on a poem, The Star, written by Jane Taylor. So how did the little poem from Essex go on to become one of the world's most recognised songs?

Jane was the daughter of writer, artist and inventor, Isaac Taylor. Her poem The Star was first featured in a book Rhymes for the Nursery in 1806 when she was living in Suffolk. Later on she lived in Colchester and then in Chipping Ongar, the place where she died and with which she is most associated.

The five stanza poem went on to be turned into a song sung to the tune of the French melody Ah! vous dirai-je, Maman. While we'll probably never know the complete story of how the poem became one of the most recognised nursery rhymes in the world, its popularity seems set to continue. Sadly, Twinkle Twinkle Little Star goes largely uncredited to Jane Tayor. Yet, it lives on. Since it was first crafted by a writer from Essex, the poem and its song version have been parodied and covered by Lewis Carroll, Leonard Nimoy and the Girl Scouts of the USA, among others!

An excerpt from John Noakes & Mary Styles; or, "An Essex calfs" visit to Tiptree races:

A poem, exhibiting some of the most striking lingual localisms peculiar to Essex. With a glossary by CHARLES CLARK, OF GREAT TOTHAM HALL, ESSEX, PUBLISHED 1839

At Tottum's Cock-a-Bevis Hill,
A sput suppass'd by few,
Where toddlers ollis haut to eye
The proper pritty wiew ;

Where people crake so ov the place,
Leas-ways, so I've hard say ;
An' rrum its top yow, sarteny,
Can see a monsus way.

'Bout this oad Hill, I warrant ya,
Their bog it nuver ceases ;
They'd growl shud yow nut own that it
Beats Danbury's au'to pieces.

But no sense ov a place, some think,
Is this here hill so high,-
Cos there, full oft, 'tis nation coad,
But that don't argufy.

Yit, if they their inquirations maake
In winter time, some will
Condemn that place as no great shakes.
Where folks ha' the coad-chill I

As sum'dy, 'haps, when nigh the sput,

May ha' a wish to see't,-
From Mauldon toun to Keldon 'tis,
An' 'gin a four releet.

Where up the road the load it goos
So lugsome an' so stiff,
That hosses mosly kitch a whop,
Frum drivers in a tiff.

But who'd pay a hoss when tugging on ?
None but a tetchy elf :
'Tis right on plain etch chap desarves
A clumsy thump himself.

Haul'd o'er the coals, sich fellars e'er
Shud be, by Martin's Act ;
But, then, they're rayther muggy oft,
So with um we're not zact.

But thussins, 'haps, to let urn oaf
Is wrong, becos etch carter,
If maade to smart, his P's and Q's
He'd mine for ever arter.

At Cock-a-Bevis Hill, too, the
Wiseacres show a tree,

Which if yow clamber up, besure,
A precious way yow see.

I dorn't think I cud clime it now,
Aldoe I uster cud ;
I shudn't warsley loike to troy,
For guelch cum down I shud.

My head 'ood swim,-I 'oodn't do' it
Nut even for a guinea :
A naarbour ax'd me, tother day,
" Naa, naa," says I, " nut quinny,'

At Cock-a-Bevis Hill, I was
A-goon to tell the folks,
Some warses back - when I bargun -
In peace there lived John Noakes.

Ees, John a bee'un foun' upon
That cried-up sput, - and I
Have hard he there lived under one
Who foliar' d husbandry.

The cot, a yard it had, in shape
A sort ov a three square ;
An' as for weeds or Utters, oh !

Yow nuver saa urn there.

No, nut in the time John's dad it hued,
Though 'twas to some a puzzle, -
'Cos long 'fore he the buekit kick'd,
He e'er was arter guzzle.

Had the ol' bouy nut yarn'd a deal,
An' fortun met him smilin', -
He'd sieh a family, he coon't
Ha' brote up the whole biling.

Who are in the warld well to do,
They onny shud ha' cubs ;
Who's nut, lore ! how he's hamper'd up,
As through this life he grubs.

Youn' John seem'd nut at all to be
A chip ov the ol' block :
To see some wet their whissles so,
It oft gave him a shock.

Through tippling in his manners, John,
No hole he'd maade at all -
(Some naarbours sed) - sen long afore
His dad lay by the wall.

No, had yow 'quired his charriter,
As people sometimes shud ;
Frum those who know'd him, yow'd bin toad
'Twas altogither gud.

To doe his jarney at the plough,
With boddle an' with bag,
Etch moarn he'd sturt some time afore
The grass was dry frum dag.

He sich a dapster was at plough,
Few match' d him nigh or far :
Ees, jes to rights, my bouys, John Noakes ,
The thurrars he 'ood draa !

But at all jobs he handy was,
He'd sich a knack at wark ;
Where'er he sew, or rep, or mew,
Yow werry soon cud mark.

No aukard, hulking fellar John,
He starr'd with nimble pace;
Nor yit bad lookin', for he had
A chubby, smilin' face.

The old mill at Burnham-on-Crouch

The Trip to Tiptree; Or, The Lover's Triumph.

Humbly presented to the Philologist as a specimen
of the dialect of the peasantry of Essex

By CHARLES CLARK

Dated Great Totham Hall, near Tiptree, Essex,
February, 1842. In Essex dialect
Sung to the tune The Teetotaller

> *Youn' Simon of Tiptree, a noice steady lad was he,*
> *The jouy ov his mother – the proide ov his dad was he ;*
> *An', as a ploughmun, folks say, yow scace ever ded*

Clap oyes upon one wot his wark hafe so clever ded.

To "come oup" to him, all his mates, they bestirrers wor,
For straight – proper straight uns – they spied all his
thurrars wor ; But our Simon, nut onny at ploughin'
excel dod he, - If he sew, rep, or mew, stell the same, oh!
so well ded he.

Stroun' an' clunchy was Simon, an' noice carlly hair
he had, With health's tints on his chakes, through the
dale ov fresh air he had : With a charriter gud, ne'er lack
"dubs" in his puss ded he, - Ollis "bobbish" an' gay, long
pass his loife thus ded he.

Howmsoever this genus - this lad ov ability –
Soon foun' a sad stup put to all his tranquillity ;
For into his heart soon much fudder loves arrars went,
Thun into the mouls e'er the teeth ov his hurrars went!

All the cause ov his troubles, 'twas werry soon sin, they
say, - He had so fell in love with one fair Dorcas Winn,
they say ; Such a noice gal was Dorcas, the chaps all
look'd sloy at her, An', poor Simon, he too, had oft caist
a ship's oye at her.

Quoite the priode ov oad Tiptree this naarbour's gud

darter was, Whoile for some toime our Simon's wesh to "goo arter" was; An' that what cud nut be at some other places done, Was – an' nut so wusser – soon at Tiptree Races done!

Nation plased now was Simon – his sithin' was banish'd quoite; To his gal he'd "struck oup" an', his fares, they had wanish'd quoite: His Dorcas's conduct, oh! now it was such he ded E'en begin to hev thotes ov the axin' at chutch, he ded!

Our Simon an' Dorcas stell yit on the Heath wor they- Now sot down in some "Tavin" 'neath the floral wreath wor they: Weher there was such guzzlin', and such ham-an-wealin' it- Whoile many loike blazes kept on toe-an-heelin' it.

What were the Tiptree Races?

As we've seen already, the Tiptree Races were once a big part of Essex life. But what were the Tiptree races and why did they matter so much to Essex people? The main association most of us have with Tiptree and Essex these days is that the village is home to the world famous brand of preserves made there by Wilkin & Sons. Yet long ago, Tiptree or rather, Tiptree Heath, was a scene of pony races.

These were a festive occasion with stalls and fun activities for locals. Right up until this century, more than 2000 acres of Tiptree Heath was open and uncultivated. While the Tiptree Races are long gone, Tiptree Heath is now the largest surviving piece of heathland in Essex and a site of special scientific interest.

Southend-on-Sea: miles of history

Southend-on-Sea has been a special part of Essex for many years. That's no surprise with it being home to the longest pier in the world at 1.34 miles! In the World War One, the popular resort was hit by one of the first air raids, with bombs from giant Zeppelins. In the Second World War, it was transformed from a popular seaside resort to a centre for the Navy, called HMS Westcliff.

A day out at the seaside: Pier Hill at Southend, showing the pier and the pier pavilion in around 1893

Kasza/ShutterStock

Strange but true: cheetah racing in Romford

Romford became the talk of Essex and the rest of the world in December 1937 thanks to a plan to organise cheetah racing in the town! There has been some discussion since about whether this bizarre idea was actually put into action. But newspaper records prove that cheetahs were actually raced around a track in Romford! Archer Leggett, the founder of the Romford Greyhound Stadium, was the man behind the unusual decision to bring cheetah racing to England. The 12 'tame' cheetahs were brought over from Kenya. They were kept in quarantine for six months before being trained at Staines and Harringay racing sites. Naturally, there were of a number of practical problems with encouraging cheetahs to run after an electric hare. The cheetahs couldn't race together because their pack instincts meant that once one animal had established itself as the 'leader', the rest would drop behind! Another of the many practical issues was that a piece of meat would have to be attached to the 'hare' for the cheetahs to take an interest in it!

The big night itself drew a big crowd. While no betting was allowed on the three races featuring cheetahs, there were lots of secret bets on the cats at very short odds! Despite the big turn out and star performances from the cheetahs (who beat their canine rivals), the idea did not take off! Read more about it at: **http://trove.nla.gov.au/ndp/del/article/11142477**

Borley Rectory: the 'most haunted house in England'?

Essex is the source of many creepy stories about what is famously said to be the "most haunted house in England"! Anyone with an interest in the supernatural will have heard of Borley Rectory. Now no longer in existence, the Victorian mansion became a source of terrifying tales, both in Essex and much further afield! Borley Rectory was built in 1863, on the site of a previous rectory, and destroyed by fire in 1939. It quickly developed a reputation throughout Essex for being a source of spooky happenings after residents had some strange experiences. Borley Rectory then went on to become the talk of the world after reports of strange phenomena such as unexplained footsteps, the ghost of a nun, ringing bells and spirit messages!

In the 1940s, the paranormal investigations into Borley Rectory were discredited. However, the reputation of the place continues. It may have burned down in 1939, but to this day, Borley Rectory in Essex remains known as 'the most haunted house in England'.

Sssh! Essex's not so 'secret' bunker

Did you know that Essex is home to a not so 'secret' bunker? Many people already do. Kelvedon Hatch Secret Nuclear Bunker in the Essex Borough of Brentwood is now a popular museum and tourist attraction in the heart of the Essex countryside. But it was once a secret location designed to protect government and other officials in the event of a nuclear war!

Despite being encased in 10 foot thick reinforced concrete and located 75 feet underground, the bunker was successfully built in complete secrecy and locals had no idea what was hidden close by! They were told that the construction work was for an underground reservoir.

The bunker was originally designed for 600 military and civilian staff, including a spot for the Prime Minister of the day! It was first an RAF ROTOR Station, then a civil defence centre before becoming a regional Government HQ.

Fortunately with the end of the cold war, the bunker was no longer needed. It was on stand-by for 30 years, costing up to £3 million pounds a year! It was decommissioned in 1992 and went into private ownership, becoming a museum and visitor attraction.

Now Kelvedon Hatch is open to visitors who can see everything from the secret entrance to the canteen! The bunker has its own water supply and electricity generators, a BBC studio, a radar room and a scientists' room.

But Kelvedon Hatch isn't the only non-secret secret bunker in Essex! It seems that the county is home to no less than five cold war control rooms!

The words behind Essex history

The Kelvedon Wonder is the famous pea that hails from Kelvedon in Essex. Jam is also a big part of the area's history with Essex being known today as the 'jam capital of Britain'! If you want to use a special ingredient in your cooking, you might treat yourself to some very special, but very costly saffron. This spice actually takes its name from Saffron Walden, the Essex village where the Saffron Crocus was once grown!

If you talked about **"Parker's Cement"** in the past, you would have been referring to Roman Cement, which became a very important industry in Harwich. Roman cement was made from septaria, hard stone-like substances in London clay. The name Parker's Cement came from the person who patented the manufacturing process in the 1700s, James Parker. Parker's cement was then overtaken by Portland cement, but this in turn gave jobs to people in

Essex through the chalk quarries at Saffron Walden. Essex was also an important centre for brick-making.

The county's name for brewing and malting was established by 1900 with Romford, Chelmsford, and Colchester being the main places involved in these activities. Corn milling was also important in Chelmsford and Colchester and in Maldon, with milling in general being a big part of Essex's history. Today, Essex is home to household names such as **Ford, Britvic, GEC Marconi and Ridleys**.

The geography of Essex also gave it a name for industry through its coastline, thanks to fishing, shipbuilding and trading. You once would have seen goods of all kinds brought into the Essex coastline on Thames Sailing Barges.

A modern-day Thames Sailing Barge in the Blackwater Estuary
Helen Shorey/Shutterstock

Workers at the steam mill and maltings at Great Bardfield
pause for a photograph in around 1885

If you'd talked about wool many years ago, Essex would have
been the name that sprang to mind. The county was closely
associated with wool and the making of woollen goods for
several centuries. It is believed that Essex and wool go back
as far as the Roman and Saxon ages. In fact, Essex was
exporting wool to Italy in the 1200s. This reputation for
textiles grew even further in the 1400s when cloth-workers
from Bruges settled in Braintree, Halstead and Dedham.

From 1550 and 1600, Colchester and nearby areas became
home to weavers and clothmakers. Their speciality was
creating Bays and Says - cloths woven from wool. During
this period Colchester was one of the most prosperous

wool towns in England. Essex was also once a big centre for textiles with the lace and silk weaving industries. If you talked about Bockings, you were referring to baize, a woollen textile, named after Bocking, the Essex town known for producing it.

Courtaulds has long been associated with textiles. It has also long been linked with Essex. The company first started in 1794 at Pebmarsh in north Essex. By 1810, the owner's son Samuel Courtauld was running a silk mill in Braintree, Essex. The company also went to run mills in other parts of Essex, providing valuable employment for local people. Courtaulds then developed an international reputation for producing crape which was used in Victorian mourning clothes. Braintree also became famous for producing the robe of cloth-of-gold for King Edward VII and the purple velvet robe for Queen Alexandra, worn at their coronation!

The railways brought big developments to Essex. In fact, some of the lines ended up leading to the creation of the holiday resorts Frinton-on-Sea, Clacton and Southend! It has to be said that the railways weren't all good news for Essex. They brought increased competition for products from other regions.

Say what? Surprising facts about Essex

Families enjoy a day out on the beach at Southend

Colchester was the capital of Roman Britain and is also Britain's oldest recorded town.

Essex is the site of the oldest church in England - St Peter's Chapel in Bradwell-on-Sea, built in 654.

Essex is home to the oldest timber framed building in the world, the Barley Barn at Cressing Temple, believed to date back to 1206.

Colchester has 1½ miles of Roman wall and it is also the oldest town wall in Britain!

Tilbury in Essex is where Queen Elizabeth I made her famous speech to soldiers preparing to fight the Spanish invasion: "I know I have the body of a weak, feeble woman; but I have the heart and stomach of a king - and of a king of England too, and think foul scorn that Parma or Spain, or any prince of Europe, should dare to invade the borders of my realm".

Tilbury Fort, near West Tilbury where **Elizabeth I** made her famous speech
S.m.u.d.g.e. /Shutterstock

Six cockle boats from Leigh-on-Sea played a crucial role in Operation Dynamo to rescue the troops from Dunkirk in World War II. Their crews succeeded in saving over 1,000 men.

The estuary of the
rivers Chelmer and
Blackwater at Maldon
in modern times
David Hughes/Shutterstock

Colchester Castle is not only older than the Tower of London, it was actually the inspiration behind its design!

Essex has the longest coastline in the UK - it's 350 miles long!

Manningtree in Essex is Britain's smallest town.

Essex is the second most heavily populated county in England with no less than 1.36 million people living there.

Greensted Church in Essex dates from the 11th century and is thought to be not only Britain's oldest wooden church, but possibly the oldest wooden church in the world.

The first crocodile transported into the UK was brought to Essex! The special visitor was brought over in 1701 by Richard Bradley who kept it in a lake at his home in Braintree.

Acknowledgements

I would like to thank Essex Record Office and the London Borough of Barking and Dagenham Archive and Local Studies Centre for their help with my research for this book and for the use of photographs from their collections.